D0825948

Sixteen Years in Sixteen Seconds

The Sammy Lee Story

For my family: Young and Kim Yoo, David Yoo, and Kyle McCorkle—P.Y.

To the first generation of Koreans who accomplished the American Dream—D.L.

Acknowledgments

I would like to acknowledge and thank Dr. Sammy Lee for his generous time and inspirational life story. Special thanks also to my editor, Philip Lee, Steven Malk of The Writers House, Dom and Keunhee Lee, Anne Park, Sandy Tanaka, Janie Bynum, Carolyn Crimi, Kelly DiPucchio, April Young Fritz, Hope Vestergaard, and Lisa Wheeler—P.Y.

Author Sources

Ku, Beulah. "Sammy Lee—Olympic Pioneer." *Asian Week*, vol. 13, no. 47 (July 17, 1992): 11.
Lee, Sammy. "An Olympians Oral History: Sammy Lee." Interview by Dr. Margaret Costa.
    Amateur Athletics Foundation of Los Angeles (December, 1999).
    http://www.aafla.com/6oic/OralHistory/OHlee.indd.pdf
Wampler, Molly Frick. *Not Without Honor: The Story of Sammy Lee*. Santa Barbara: The
    Fithian Press, 1987.

Text copyright © 2005 by Paula Yoo
Illustrations copyright © 2005 by Dom Lee

All rights reserved. No part of the contents of this book may be reproduced by any means without the written permission of the publisher.
LEE & LOW BOOKS Inc., 95 Madison Avenue, New York, NY 10016
leeandlow.com

Manufactured in China by South China Printing Co., January 2010

Book design by David Neuhaus/NeuStudio
Book production by The Kids at Our House

The text is set in New Aster
The illustrations are rendered by applying acrylic color on paper, melting encaustic beeswax over it, scratching the images out of the wax, and then adding colored pencil and oil.

(HC) 10 9 8 7 6 5
(PB) 10 9 8 7 6 5 4 3 2 1
First Edition

Library of Congress Cataloging-in-Publication Data
Yoo, Paula.
    Sixteen years in sixteen seconds : the Sammy Lee story / by Paula Yoo ; illustrations by Dom Lee. — 1st ed.
    p. cm.
    ISBN 978-1-58430-247-6 (hardcover)   ISBN 978-1-60060-453-9 (paperback)
1. Lee, Sammy, 1920—Juvenile literature. 2. Divers—United States—Biography—Juvenile literature. 3. Springboard diving—Juvenile literature. I. Lee, Dom, 1959- ill. II. Title.
GV838.L44Y66 2005
797.2'4'092—dc22   [B]   2004020962

Sixteen Years in Sixteen Seconds

The Sammy Lee Story

WITHDRAWN

by Paula Yoo • illustrations by Dom Lee

Lee & Low Books Inc.
New York

The sign at the swimming pool read, MEMBERS ONLY.

Twelve-year-old Sammy Lee knew exactly what that sign meant— only whites were permitted to enter even though it was a public pool. This was the practice in 1932. Sammy would have to wait until Wednesday, when people of color were allowed to go inside. In the meantime, he would get no relief from the blazing California summer sun.

Sammy clutched the chain-link gate. He gazed in envy at the children splashing and shouting in the water. He watched as a boy stood on the diving board and held out his arms. The boy flew high in the air and broke the surface of the water with hardly a splash.

I want to learn how to do that, Sammy thought.

The following Wednesday, Sammy was the first one through the open gate. He raced to the springboard, stood on the edge, and spread his arms like wings. He took a deep breath and leaped as high as he could.

Sammy soared. *I'm flying*, he thought. He tucked his knees against his chest and spun into a somersault.

SPLAT!

Sammy splashed everyone, including his friend Hart Crum, who was also limited to using the pool on Wednesdays because he was African American.

Hart challenged Sammy to do more than one somersault. Sammy, eager to show off, raced back to the springboard. Try as he might, Sammy could only complete one somersault.

Hart stopped teasing Sammy and offered to help him instead. He followed Sammy onto the diving board and together they jumped. When they landed, Hart's extra weight helped Sammy leap higher into the air. This time Sammy completed one-and-a-half somersaults before hitting the water! He grinned, eager to practice again with Hart.

Over the summer, Sammy discovered he had a natural talent for diving, but his father wanted him to stop wasting time with sports and instead become a doctor. Sammy's parents had left Korea for a better life in America. His father worked hard at their family's restaurant, saving money in the bank and putting his tips in a shoe box for his son's future. "In America," Sammy's father said, "you can achieve anything if you set your heart to it."

One morning Sammy and his father drove to the market downtown to pick up vegetables for their restaurant. The streets were lined with flags from different countries. Sammy's father explained that Los Angeles was hosting the Olympics and the flags represented the participating countries. The gold medal winners were considered the greatest athletes in the world.

A chill ran through Sammy. Although his father wanted him to be a doctor, Sammy knew he wanted to be an Olympic champion.

Sammy decided that diving would be his ticket to the Olympics, but he knew sooner or later he would have to find a coach to help him improve his diving skills. He couldn't just rely on his friend Hart giving him advice.

In the summer of 1938, when he was eighteen, Sammy attended a swim and diving competition. Between meets he sneaked into the pool area to practice. When Sammy came up for air after his first dive, he heard one of the coaches shout, "That's the lousiest dive I've ever seen!"

Sammy spotted a tall, heavyset man at the edge of the pool. "You get back up there and practice until I say you can quit," the man barked. "Stand straight! Spread your arms out more! Your arch is too deep!"

Sammy wondered why this stranger was suddenly giving him orders. He obeyed anyway, curious to see if the man's advice would help improve his dives. By the end of the day, Sammy was exhausted, but he had never dived better.

"I'm Jim Ryan," the man finally said. "I'm your new coach."

Because Sammy could only use the local pool one day a week, Coach Ryan had him dig a giant hole in the coach's backyard. They filled this pit with sand and installed a diving board above it.

Sammy trained every day in that sandpit. The gritty sand filled his ears, and his palms were lined with grime. When it rained, the wet sand weighed down his swimming trunks. Once Sammy slipped and cut his forehead, but he didn't give up. He never disobeyed Coach Ryan's endless orders.

To keep from hurting himself, Sammy had to land on his feet after each dive into the sandpit. So he enrolled in a gymnastics class at school to help develop stronger leg muscles. As a result, Sammy was able to jump much higher off the diving board than other divers. Performing difficult dives became easy for him, and Sammy earned a reputation for his graceful and seemingly effortless dives.

Although Sammy was exhausted every night from a full day of school followed by diving practice and homework, he managed to keep up his grades and earn all As. Sammy's classmates voted him Most Likely to Succeed, and he was the first nonwhite student elected as student body president. Occidental College in Los Angeles, impressed with Sammy's achievements, offered him a full scholarship.

Despite his academic and athletic success, Sammy still faced discrimination. During his senior year of high school, Sammy could not attend his own prom. It was held at the Pasadena Civic Auditorium, and only white students were allowed to enter.

That injustice angered Sammy. How could his father insist that Sammy could achieve anything in America when he wasn't even allowed to attend his own prom?

Diving was the only world where Sammy felt he belonged. Even though he had graduated at the top of his high school class, his grades dropped during his first year of college because he spent more time diving than studying.

Sammy and his father fought over his grades. Sammy didn't understand why his father refused to support his dream of becoming an Olympic champion.

Then one afternoon Sammy witnessed a rude customer berating his father at the restaurant. Later Sammy asked his father how he could allow people to treat him that way. His father answered that instead of losing his temper, he acted with honor. He explained that if Sammy became a doctor, he would get the respect he deserved. "In America, you can achieve anything if you set your heart to it," he reminded Sammy.

For the first time, Sammy understood why his father pressured him to do well in school. So he struck a deal with him. Sammy could dive as long as his grades were good enough for medical school.

While studying to be a doctor, Sammy continued to enter diving competitions. He hoped to qualify for the next Olympic Games in Helsinki, Finland, but because of World War II, the 1940 Olympics were canceled. Sammy was crushed. He thought his dream of becoming an Olympic champion had ended.

In 1943 Sammy's father suffered a heart attack and died. Sammy was devastated. Then he remembered his father's shoe box—the one filled with money for Sammy's future. He could not let his father's dream die.

Sammy took a break from diving and worked hard to get accepted into a special United States Army medical training program. He discovered he did have a passion for medicine and became a doctor in 1946.

Sammy started working at different hospitals in California, but he missed diving. So he found a pool near each hospital and practiced diving after his shifts ended. Still dreaming of the Olympics, Sammy entered the national diving championship in 1946. Even though he did not have much time to train for the event, Sammy won the high-platform dive with the highest score ever.

Despite his achievements, Sammy continued to face discrimination. Once, after performing at a diving exhibition with his friends, Sammy was forbidden from entering a restaurant to have dinner with them. And Sammy was still restricted from using some pools except on assigned days.

Instead of getting angry over such unfair treatment, Sammy decided to prove his worth at the upcoming 1948 Olympic Games in London. He received special permission from the army to take off time for training.

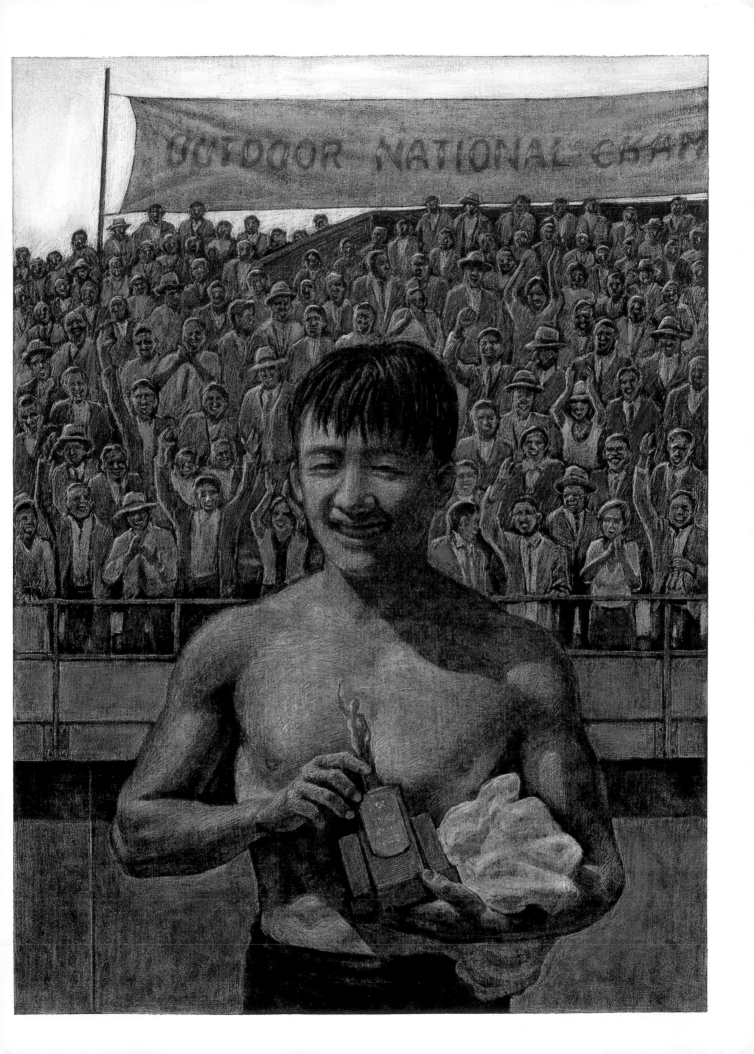

At the age of twenty-eight, Sammy qualified to be a member of the U.S. Olympic diving team. The diving competition was held at the Empire Pool in Wembley Stadium in London. Sammy was in awe as he entered the stadium. Here he was, the son of Korean immigrants, representing the United States at the Olympics. He knew his family would be proud.

Sammy's first diving event was the 3-meter springboard dive. He was nervous, and the excitement was almost unbearable. At previous competitions, Sammy would usually put lamb's wool in his ears to block out the noise of the crowd so he could concentrate. But Sammy was finally at the Olympics. He didn't want to miss a thing. He took out his earplugs so he could hear everything.

Sammy stood on the diving board. He was sure everyone could hear his heart beating. Then he focused himself, jumped high, and made one of his best dives ever. It won him the bronze medal.

Sammy was happy but not satisfied. He wanted to win a gold medal. He knew his strength lay in the upcoming 10-meter platform event. Here was his chance to show he was the greatest diver in the world.

Right before the event, Sammy heard a rumor that there might be some prejudice against him because he wasn't white. This only added to his determination to win.

Sammy remained calm. "I'm going for the gold," he told his teammates before climbing up the ladder. He no longer wanted to win just for himself. He wanted to win to prove that no one should be judged by the color of his or her skin.

For his final dive in the 10-meter platform event, Sammy decided to perform the forward three-and-a-half somersault. This was a very dangerous move. The slightest miscalculation in timing could lead to a serious, even fatal, injury.

Sammy faced a crowd of thousands. His mouth was dry. He heard the sound of water lapping against the sides of the pool, the murmuring of the people, the beating of his heart.

Never before had Sammy felt such intense pressure. He had trained sixteen years for this—a moment that would last barely sixteen seconds from the time he dived to when the scores would be revealed.

Sammy closed his eyes, and in his mind he was twelve years old again. It was Wednesday at the pool. He and Hart were practicing somersaults. Somehow, this image calmed Sammy's nerves. He opened his eyes, took a deep breath, and leaped off the edge of the platform.

Sammy flew through the air. He did one . . . then two . . . then three . . . and a half somersaults!

The crowd gasped.

As Sammy surfaced, drops of water trickled over his eyes. He shook his head and blinked. Then he saw the scores.

7.0
9.0
9.5
9.5
9.5
9.5

And then . . . 10.0. Ten! He had a perfect score!

Sammy Lee was an Olympic champion.

Sammy stood on the podium as the United States flag was raised high. *I did it*, he thought, beaming with pride. He had won the gold medal, not only for himself, but for his father, Coach Ryan, and Hart Crum. He had also won the gold for his country. Someday, he hoped, all swimming pools would be open every day of the week for all Americans.

The crowd roared. Voices filled the cavernous stadium, but all Sammy could hear were his father's words: "In America, you can achieve anything if you set your heart to it."

Author's Note

Sammy Lee was born on August 1, 1920, in Fresno, California, the youngest child of SoonKee and EunKee Chun Rhee. They later moved to Highland Park, California, where Sammy grew up with his two older sisters, Dolly and Mary.

Although Sammy always dreamed of being an Olympic champion, he first followed his father's dream of becoming a doctor. Finally, at age twenty-eight, he also made his own dream come true. At the 1948 Olympic Games in London, England, Dr. Sammy Lee became the first Asian American to win a gold medal. He won the gold medal in the 10-meter platform diving event and the bronze medal in the 3-meter springboard event.

After the 1948 Olympics, Sammy Lee served as a doctor in the Korean War. Then, at the 1952 Olympic Games in Helsinki, Finland, Dr. Lee became the first man ever to defend an Olympic platform-diving title. He was also the first male diver to win gold medals for diving in two consecutive Olympics.

In 1953 Sammy Lee was the first Asian American awarded the James E. Sullivan Award. This award is given annually by the Amateur Athletic Union to the top amateur athlete in the United States. It is considered the most prestigious sports award in the country. Dr. Lee later coached diver Bob Webster to Olympic gold medals in 1960 and 1964, and Greg Louganis to a silver medal at the 1976 Olympic Games. Today, at eighty-four years old, Dr. Sammy Lee is still an active athlete. He lives in California with his wife, Rosalind. They have two children and three grandchildren.

Paula Yoo, 2004

31901047219664